C000319596

Recipe Notes

All spoon measures are level: 1 tablesp
1 teaspoon = 5ml spoon.

Follow EITHER metric or Imperial measures and NEVER mix
in one recipe as they are not interchangeable.

Eggs used are a medium size 3 unless otherwise stated.

Kilojoules and kilocalories at the end of each recipe are
represented by the letters kj and kcal.

This edition published 1994 by Merehurst Limited
Ferry House, 51-57 Lacy Road,
Putney, London SW15 1PR

Copyright © Gräfe und Unzer GmbH 1993, Munich

ISBN 1 874567 31 X

Designed by Clive Dorman & Co.
Printed in Italy by G. Canale & C.S.p.A

Distributed in the UK by J.B. Fairfax Press Limited,
9 Trinity Centre, Park Farm, Wellingborough, Northants NN8 6ZB

Distributed in Australia by J.B. Fairfax Press Pty Ltd,
80 McLachlan Avenue, Rushcutters Bay, Sydney, NSW 2011

Raspberry Fluff

Serves 10

Light and cool, ideal for a birthday pudding. A child's age made from fruit makes a spectacular finishing touch.

Preparation time: about 45 minutes, plus 2 hours chilling

CRUST
185g (6oz) digestive biscuits
60g (2oz) caster sugar
1 teaspoon cinnamon
75g (2½ oz) margarine

FILLING
1 packet raspberry jelly
155ml (5fl oz/⅔ cup) boiling water
425g (15oz) can of raspberries in syrup
175ml (6fl oz/¾ cup) evaporated milk, chilled overnight
3 teaspoons lemon juice
Fresh raspberries for decoration
1 tablespoon rolled porridge oats
Fresh mint leaves for decoration

1 To make crust, crush biscuits and put into mixing bowl. Toss in sugar and cinnamon. Melt margarine. Add to biscuit mixture and mix well with fork. Press biscuit crumbs over base and sides of 23cm (9in) glass pie plate or flan dish. Chill for 1 hour to set.

2 Divide jelly into cubes, put into saucepan, add water and melt over low heat. Add 60ml (2fl oz/¼ cup) syrup from can of fruit. Leave to cool then chill until just beginning to thicken and set. The jelly should have the consistency of unbeaten egg white.

3 Drain raspberries thoroughly, reserving juice for drinks or fruit salads. Whip evaporated milk and lemon juice together in mixing bowl until fluffy and very thick.

4 Gradually whisk thickened jelly into evaporated milk mixture then quickly and gently fold in raspberries. Spoon into crumb crust and chill for about 2 hours until set and firm.

5 Before serving, decorate top edge of flan with fresh raspberries and sides with oats. Arrange more raspberries in shape of child's age and decorate with mint leaves. Cut into portions with a wet knife to stop jelly mixture from sticking.

Nutritional value per portion:
about 1300kj/310kcal
Protein: 13g
Fat: 14g
Carbohydrate: 31g

Raspberry Fluff

Double Deckers

Makes 4

Yummy little sandwich cakes to delight any child.

Preparation time: about 20 minutes

1 ready-made Jamaica ginger cake or
   golden syrup cake
155ml (5fl oz/⅔ cup) whipping cream
1 teaspoon vanilla essence
1 teaspoon finely grated lemon rind
75g (2½ oz) blackcurrant or cherry jam
2 teaspoons icing sugar

1 Put cake on to board, unwrap and cut lengthwise into 4 long strips. Using a 6cm (2½ in) round pastry cutter, cut out 2 rounds from each strip of cake.

2 Pour cream into mixing bowl, add vanilla essence and whip until cream is thick.

3 Fold in lemon rind and jam, gently stirring with large spoon until well combined.

4 Sandwich rounds of cake together, in pairs, with cream mixture.

5 Sift over icing sugar just before serving

TIP
Use cake trimmings for trifle.

Nutritional value per serving:
about 1900kJ/450kcal
Protein: 10g
Fat: 28g
Carbohydrate: 39g

Double Deckers

Fruit Tartlet Puffs

Makes 24

Puff pastry cases with a light creamy filling and delicious fruit topping.

Preparation time: about 35 minutes

24 medium-sized frozen vol-au-vent cases
1 egg, beaten
155ml (5fl oz/$^2/_3$ cup) whipping cream
155g (5oz) full-fat soft cheese, at room
   temperature
1 tablespoon milk
6 teaspoons caster sugar
625g (1$^1/_4$ lb) mixed fresh summer fruits
30g (1oz) jelly glaze mix
220ml (7fl oz/1 cup) cold water

1 Put frozen vol-au-vent cases on to 2 ungreased baking trays, placing them 2.5cm (1in) apart. Brush rims with beaten egg and bake in oven as directed on packet.

2 Transfer cooked vol-au-vents to cooling racks and push down soft middles gently with back of teaspoon. Cool pastry cases completely.

3 To make filling, place cream in mixing bowl and whip until thick. In separate bowl, beat cheese with milk until smooth. Fold in cream alternately with sugar.

4 Spoon equal amounts of filling into vol-au-vent cases then cover with soft fruit. Finally, spoon over jelly glaze mix, made up as directed on packet.

TIPS
For alternatives to vol-au-vents, try the following:
1 Ready-made puff pastry cases in assorted shapes as shown in picture.
2 Individual sponge flan cases.
3 Ready-made or home-made meringue nests.
4 Ready-made brandy snap baskets.

Nutritional value of each vol-au-vent:
about 500kj/120kcal
Protein: 5g
Fat: 6g
Carbohydrate: 14g

Fruit Tartlet Puffs

Berry Jelly

Serves 6

Children will love this impressive moulded fruit jelly.

Preparation time: about 40 minutes , plus 5 hours setting

½ packet raspberry jelly
½ packet strawberry jelly
½ packet pineapple jelly
250g (8oz) mixed fresh raspberries and
    strawberries

1 Divide raspberry and strawberry jelly into cubes and put into large measuring jug.

2 Make jelly up to 500ml (16fl oz/2 cups) with water. Melt as directed on the packet then pour into mixing bowl.

3 Leave jelly to stand until cold then cover with plate and chill until just beginning to thicken and set.

4 Make up pineapple jelly as directed on packet. Pour into shallow dish and chill until set.

5 Meanwhile rinse fruit, drain thoroughly and reserve a strawberry halve for decoration. Stir fruit into half-set berry jelly then spoon into medium-sized, wetted jelly mould. Cover loosely with non-stick baking paper and chill for 5 hours until set.

6 Before serving, tip pineapple jelly on to piece of dampened non-stick baking paper placed on chopping board. Chop into tiny cubes with wetted round-bladed knife.

7 Unmould fruit jelly on to serving plate and surround with chopped pineapple jelly cubes. Decorate with strawberry halve and serve in dessert dishes.

Nutritional value per portion:
about 530kJ/130kcal
Protein: 4g
Fat: negligible
Carbohydrate: 27g

Berry Jelly

Penny Pizzas

Makes 21

Delicious little morsels for children of all ages.

Preparation time: about 1 hour

BASE
280g (9oz) packet Pizza Base Mix

TOPPING
2 tablespoons olive oil
185g (6oz) passata or tomato purée
Garlic salt to taste
Freshly milled black pepper to taste
7 thin slices of salami
7 cherry tomatoes
7 mushrooms
1 small courgette (zucchini), thinly sliced
60g (2oz) lean ham, cut into strips
250g (8oz) Mozzarella cheese
2 tablespoons chopped fresh parsley

1 Make up pizza base mix as directed on packet. Put on to floured work surface and divide into 21 equal-sized pieces. Roll out into rounds measuring about 3.5cm(1½ in) in diameter. Put on to large oiled baking trays. Preheat oven to 220C (425F/Gas7).

2 Mix oil and passata and spread evenly over pizza bases, leaving edges clear. Sprinkle with garlic salt and pepper.

3 Cover 7 pizzas with slices of salami. Halve tomatoes and place on top. Trim mushrooms and put on to next 7 pizzas, stalk-sides up. Finally add courgette (zucchini) slices and ham strips to remaining 7 Pizzas.

4 Grate cheese coarsely and sprinkle evenly over pizzas. Bake in oven for about 12 minutes, rearranging position of baking trays half way through cooking. Sprinkle with parsley and serve warm.

Nutritional value per pizza:
about 410kj/100cal
Protein: 5g
Fat:5g
Carbohydrate: 9g

Penny Pizzas

Sneaky Snake

Serves 6

A fun way of arranging party food.

Preparation time: about 25 minutes

1 large cucumber
1 strip of red pepper (capsicum)
2 cloves
100g (3½ oz) sliced pumpernickel or whole-
    meal bread
155g (5oz) full fat soft cheese or cheese
    spread
185g (6oz) piece of garlic sausage or other
    cooked sausage
2 small tomatoes
5 round smoked cheese slices

1 Cut tail end off cucumber to form a snake's head and make a slit in its narrowest part to resemble mouth. Cut pepper (capsicum) strip into a tongue with a centre split running almost to the top to form a forked tongue. Put tongue into snake's mouth then add 2 cloves for eyes. Put on to serving plate.

2 Cut remaining cucumber into slices. Cut pumpernickel or wholemeal bread into 5cm (2in) rounds with a pastry cutter and spread with soft cheese or cheese spread.

3 Slice sausage and tomatoes. Arrange all prepared ingredients with smoked cheese slices on plate to form a curved snake, starting at head end.

4 Alternate ingredients for colour contrast, referring to picture opposite. Allow children to eat their way through snake with their fingers.

Nutrition value per portion:
about 1100kj/260kcal
Protein: 14g
Fat: 18g
Carbohydrate: 12g

Sneaky Snake

Beano Baps

Makes 8

These seeded baps filled with ham and vegetable salad are hard to resist!

Preparation time: about 30 minutes

4 seeded bap rolls
1 tablespoon sunflower margarine

FILLING
4 cherry tomatoes
2 tablespoons chopped fresh chives
100g (3½ oz) ham
60g (2oz) canned sweetcorn, drained
155ml (5fl oz/⅔ cup) thick soured cream
Salt and pepper
8 lettuce leaves

1 Warm rolls through either in oven, microwave or under grill, then halve each.

2 Halve tomatoes and put into mixing bowl. Add chives. Cut ham into narrow strips. Add to bowl with sweetcorn and soured cream.

3 Stir tomato mixture well and season to taste with salt and pepper.

4 Spread baps with margarine, top with lettuce leaves and equal amounts of salad. Serve straight away.

TIPS
1 Chopped and crisply-grilled bacon can replace ham, as can strips of Edam cheese.
2 Coarsely chopped unpeeled red apple can be used to replace the sweetcorn.

Nutritional value per bap:
about 890kj/210kcal
Protein: 8g
Fat: 8g
Carbohydrate: 28g

Beano Baps

Step-by step

STRAWBERRY AND LEMON MILK SHAKE

1 Put 250g (8oz) natural yogurt and 250ml (8fl oz/1 cup) skimmed milk into blender. Add 500g (1lb) washed and hulled strawberries and blend until smooth.

2 Pour milk shake into 4 tumblers and add 1 or 2 scoops of lemon sorbet to each.

3 Decorate with whole or halved strawberries speared on to sticks. Add a drinking straw.

LEMONADE

4 Finely grate rind of 2 lemons. Cut rind of third lemon into spiral, keeping it in one continous piece.

5 Squeeze juice from fruit. Combine with 100g (3½ oz) clear honey. Add grated rind, cover and stand for 1 hour to bring out flavours.

6 Strain juice into jug and decorate rim with lemon rind spiral. To serve, pour into medium-sized tumblers, half filling each. Top up with sparkling mineral water.

CHILLED MELON PUNCH

7 Halve a small Ogen or Charentais melon. Remove seeds and cut out flesh using a melon baller.

8 Put flesh into large bowl. Add 1 cinnamon stick and 90ml (3fl oz/⅓ cup) unsweetened apple juice. Cover and chill for 1 hour.

9 Remove cinnamon stick. Pour l litre (1¾ pint/4 cups) lemonade over melon and stir round. Ladle into tumblers and add a drinking straw to each.

1

4

7

3

6

9

Fruit Waffles

Serves 6

You can make your own waffles if you have a waffle iron but bought ones are more convenient and taste just as good. If you are unable to find fancy-shaped waffles, like the ones shown in the picture, use square or oblong ones instead.

Preparation time: about 15 minutes

2 oranges
155ml (5fl oz/⅔ cup) whipping cream
6 teaspoons caster sugar
2 kiwi fruit
6 ready-made or home-made waffles

1 Cut skin and pith from oranges and cut into segments, cutting between the skin. Pat slices dry with absorbent kitchen paper and set aside.

2 Whip cream and sugar until thick.

3 Peel kiwi fruit thinly, halve each one lengthwise then cut each half into thin slices.

4 Reheat waffles as directed on packet, usually by toasting. Alternatively, warm through in microwave oven.

5 Put waffles on to 6 plates. Top with whipped cream then decorate with orange and kiwi slices. Serve warm.

TIPS

1 If preferred, use canned peach slices instead of fresh orange segments.
2 Add 30g (1oz) chocolate chips to cream mixture after whipping.

Nutritional value per portion:
about 2400kj/570kcal
Protein: 15g
Fat: 33g
Carbohydrate: 54g

Fruit Waffles

Funny Face Cake

Serves 12

A quick and easy novelty cake, especially if using a ready-made sponge cake.

Preparation time: about 1 hour

90g (3oz) plain (dark) chocolate
280ml (10fl oz/1¼ cups) whipping cream, chilled
20cm (8in) home-made or ready-made sandwich or sponge cake, cut into 2 layers
60g (2oz) apricot jam
3 large chocolate flake bars
2 hazelnuts
1 slice white bread, lightly toasted
1 tablespoon icing sugar
Red food colouring

1 Break up chocolate and melt in bowl standing over saucepan of gently simmering water. Alternatively, melt in microwave oven for 1-2 minutes on Medium power. Leave chocolate until just cold but still liquid.

2 Whip cream until very stiff then gradually beat in cooled, melted chocolate. Cover and chill for 30 minutes to firm up.

3 Cut each cake in half horizontally then sandwich together again with apricot jam and a little of the chocolate cream.

4 Spread remaining cream smoothly over top and sides of cake. Crush flake bars and press against sides with round-bladed knife. Using 2 spatulas, carefully lift cake on to serving plate.

5 Make eyes with hazelnuts. Cut out a triangular nose and crescent eyebrows from toast. Cut out a ring for the mouth.

6 Mix icing sugar with a few drops water and colour pale pink. Spoon onto ring to make pink lips. Arrange nose, eyebrows and lips on cake. Chill cake before serving.

Nutritional value per portion:
about 300kj/310kcal
Protein: 9g
Fat: 15g
Carbohydrate: 35g

Funny Face Cake

Date and Nut Baked Apples

Serves 6

Designed for winter parties when fresh dates start appearing in the shops.

Preparation time: about 45 minutes

Margarine for greasing
6 large fresh dates
60g (2oz) hazelnuts
½ teaspoon cinnamon, plus a little extra
6 red apples
220g (7oz) thick natural yogurt
½ teaspoon vanilla essence
6 teaspoons clear honey
125ml (4 fl oz/½ cup) whipping cream

1 Preheat oven to 220C (425F/Gas7). Lightly grease a baking tray with margarine. Skin dates, cut each in half and remove stones. Chop flesh.

2 Slowly dry-fry hazelnuts in a non-stick pan until golden, stirring frequently. Tip nuts into large cloth and rub hard between folds to remove as much skin as possible. Chop nuts and put into mixing bowl. Add dates and cinnamon.

3 Core apples with apple corer and pack hollows with date mixture. Place on prepared tray and bake in oven for 15 minutes.

4 Meanwhile, tip yogurt into small mixing bowl and stir in vanilla essence and honey. Whip cream in separate bowl until thick then gradually fold into yogurt with large metal spoon. Spoon into serving dish, sprinkle with extra cinnamon and serve with apples.

Nutritional value per portion:
about 990kj/240kcal
Protein: 2g
Fat: 13g
Carbohydrate: 29g

Date and Nut Baked Apples

Whirligigs

Makes 8

Melt-in-the-mouth!

Preparation time: about 40 minutes

185g (6oz) lightly salted butter, softened
60g (2oz) icing sugar, sifted
½ teaspoon vanilla essence
170g (5½ oz) white cake flour
15g (½ oz) cocoa powder
Orange segments for serving

FILLING
90ml (3fl oz/⅓ cup) whipping cream
2 teaspoons caster sugar
1 tablespoon shelled pistachio nuts,
   chopped

1 Butter a large baking tray. Preheat oven to 160C (325F/Gas 3).

2 Put butter, icing sugar and vanilla essence into mixing bowl and beat until light and creamy.

3 Sift flour and cocoa powder on to plate. Gradually fork into creamed butter mixture until well combined. Spoon into piping bag fitted with large star-shaped tube.

4 Pipe 16 whirls of mixture on to prepared tray. Bake in oven for about 20 minutes until light golden. Cool slightly then gently remove from tray with knife or spatula and put on to wire cooling rack.

5 Whip cream and caster sugar until thick. Stir in nuts. Sandwich biscuits together in pairs with nut cream. Serve on the day of cooking with orange segments.

TIPS
1 Instead of pistachios, use chopped walnuts or lightly toasted almond flakes.
2 You will find cake flour next to the ordinary flours in the supermarket. If preferred, use plain flour instead.

Nutritional value per pair of biscuits:
about 870kj/210kcal
Protein: 4g
Fat: 13g
Carbohydrate: 21g

Whirligigs

Party Porcupine

Serves 6

Have a stab at this one!

Preparation time: about 1 hour

1 small red or white hard cabbage
220g (7oz) Kabanos or peperoni sausage
315g (10oz) Gouda cheese, rind removed or
    Cheddar
1 medium cucumber
1 yellow pepper (capsicum)
3 small carrots
250g (8oz) cherry tomatoes
250g (8oz) pickled gherkins, drained
250g (8oz) pickled silverskin onions

1 Cut a slice off stem end of cabbage so that it stands upright. Wrap in foil and stand on large plate.

2 Cut Kabanos or peperoni into 1cm (½ in) pieces. Cut cheese into 2.5cm (1in) cubes.

3 Wash and dry cucumber. Cut into 2.5cm (1in) pieces and cut each piece into quarters. Halve pepper (capsicum) then remove inner white membranes and seeds. Cut flesh into 2.5cm (1in) squares. Peel carrots, halve each lengthwise and cut each half into 2.5cm (1in) pieces.

4 Thread all prepared ingredients alternately on to cocktail sticks interspersing them with tomatoes, gherkins and onions. Push into cabbage and serve.

Nutritional value per serving:
about 1600kj/380kcal
Protein: 20g
Fat: 31g
Carbohydrate: 7g

Party Porcupine

Baked Pancake Stack

Serves 6

A savoury cheese and egg dish which goes well with coleslaw or a mixed green salad.

Preparation time: about 1 hour

3 large eggs
185g (6oz) plain white flour, sifted
280ml (9fl oz/1 cup) cold milk
½ teaspoon salt
500g (1lb) tomatoes
250g (8oz) Mozzarella cheese
Sparkling mineral water
170g (5½ oz) crème fraîche
2 tablespoons chopped fresh chives

1 To make batter, break eggs into large mixing bowl, whisk until foamy then beat in flour alternately with milk. Season with salt.

2 Thinly slice tomatoes. Grate cheese. Preheat oven to 200C (400F/Gas 6).

3 Add a dash of mineral water to batter for extra lightness then use to make six 23cm (9in) pancakes, frying in greased frying pan.

4 Stack pancakes, as they are cooked, one on top of the other with squares of non-stick baking paper between each.

5 Fill a well-greased 20cm(8in) springform cake tin alternately with layers of pancakes, crème fraîche, chives, tomatoes and Mozzarella, starting with crème fraîche and ending with cheese.

6 Bake in oven for 30 minutes. Unclip sides of tin, cut cake into 6 portions and serve hot.

Nutritional value per portion:
about 1900kj/450kcal
Protein: 17g
Fat: 29g
Carbohydrate: 32g

Baked Pancake Stack

Potato Posies

Serves 6

Children will love these flower-shaped savouries.

Preparation time: about 50 minutes

12 even-sized small potatoes
60g (2oz) butter, melted
salt to taste
100g (3½ oz) Cheddar cheese, grated
1 tablespoon sesame seeds
1 slice wholemeal bread
1 small onion, peeled and grated
250g (8oz) lean minced beef
1 egg
Slices red pepper (capsicum), for garnishing

1 Peel and wash potatoes. Cut into paper thin slices. Preheat oven to 200C (400/Gas 6).

2 Butter 2 or 3 large baking trays. Arrange potato slices, in 12 rosettes, on prepared trays, overlapping slices slightly so they remain in place.

3 Sprinkle potatoes evenly with salt, cheese, sesame seeds and remaining melted butter.

4 For meat balls, soak bread in water until soft then squeeze dry with hands and put into mixing bowl. Add onion, beef and egg. Knead together until well combined and shape into 12 balls. Put one meatball on to centre of each rosette.

5 Bake in oven for 25-30 minutes until golden brown. Cool for 5 minutes then transfer to 6 plates with a fish slice. Decorate each meatball with a small circle of red pepper (capsicum) if liked, and serve hot.

Nutritional value per portion:
about 1700kj/400kcal
Protein: 23g
Fat: 26g
Carbohydrate: 22g

Potato Posies

Step-by step

FRUIT PUNCH

1 Put 2 bags of fruit tea into saucepan. Add 530ml (17fl oz/2 cups) boiling water. Leave for 5 minutes then remove tea bags.

2 Squeeze juice of 4 large oranges. Strain into hot tea. Sweeten with 4 teaspoons clear honey. Heat through without boiling.

3 Dip rims of 4 mugs into lemon juice then dip in brown sugar. Carefully fill with punch.

REAL HOT CHOCOLATE

4 Gently melt 100g (3½ oz) milk chocolate in saucepan with 6 teaspoons water.

5 Gradually beat in 530ml (17fl oz/2 cups) milk and continue to beat until drink is hot and foamy. Do not boil.

6 Whip 100ml (3½ fl oz) whipping cream and ½ teaspoon vanilla essence together until stiff. Pour hot chocolate into mugs and top each with cream. Sprinkle with cocoa powder.

APPLE TODDY

7 Put 4 small cooking apples on to greased tray. Sprinkle with 1 teaspoon cinnamon and bake at 200C (400F/Gas 6) for 30 minutes.

8 Put cooked apples into large pan. Add 750ml (1¼ pint/25fl oz) boiling water and blend to a purée. Rub through sieve directly into second saucepan.

9 Sprinkle 12 large brown sugar cubes with lemon juice. Drop into 4 mugs. Reheat apple drink until hot but not boiling. Pour into mugs. Decorate with canned cherries speared with cocktail sticks.